Balboa Press books may be ordered through booksellers or by contacting:

Balboa Press
A Division of Hay House
1663 Liberty Drive
Bloomington, IN 47403
www.balboapress.com
844-682-1282

Interior Image Credit: Ariane Elsammak

ISBN: 978-1-9822-7372-9 (sc)
ISBN: 979-8-7652-4717-4 (hc)
ISBN: 978-1-9822-7373-6 (e)

Library of Congress Control Number: 2021918013

Print information available on the last page.

Balboa Press rev. date: 11/15/2023

About the Author....

Douglas Macauley lives in San Francisco, California. He is a dedicated father with children spanning two generations: a daughter age twelve, and a son age thirty–two. With degrees in electrical engineering and computer science, Douglas builds on his three decades as an electrical engineer for his work as a mindfulness practitioner, life coach, and intuitive energy healer. Douglas believes mindfulness allows us to find our centers, inner peace, and harmony while being guided by our hearts and staying grounded in our truth, which ultimately leads us to live a joyful life.

I Am Grounded

A Path to Stability and Feeling Safe

By Douglas Macauley

Illustrated by Ariane Elsammak

About the Book....

Expanding upon *I Am a Feeling Body: Body Awareness and Mindfulness for Children* and focused on grounding as the first and foundational tenet for feeling a deep sense of stability and safety, *I Am Grounded* is an empowering book about a boy and his two loving cats as they explore and flow on their path, taking in the currents of each breath at every turn in their adventure. Along the way, they find challenges and obstacles that present opportunities for overcoming and embracing a new approach to freedom and safety. The playfulness and joy they experience compounds while grounding them with humility and gratitude in all they discover. Their lives become brighter, filled with greater awareness in their bodies while actualizing deeper meaning in relation to each other and those they encounter.

For my dear children,
Mark and Madelyn:

Life grows more meaningful and joyous every
day as you both fill my heart with love.
I am deeply grateful for having you in my life.

And in memory of and with deep gratitude for
my sweet and loving cats, Licorice and Taffi,
who always embodied unconditional love.

Note to Parents....

Grounding is the first of four essential tenets in creating a solid foundation to instill ongoing peace, harmony, happiness, and well-being in our lives. As described in my first book, *I Am a Feeling Body: Body Awareness and Mindfulness for Children,* these tenets include grounding, centering, breathing, and feeling as they relate directly to awareness of and connection with the body.

This book focuses on grounding as fundamental for the body to feel connected with all that is. Our awareness of how we feel becomes a critical first step to instilling a solid connection between mind and body. When we invite ourselves to feel what is going on inside the body, and as our awareness spreads, we can anchor in two primary components of grounding. One is feeling grounded with the earth underneath us, and the other is feeling an evolving wholeness that constitutes all our body parts working as an integrated, flowing, spacious container that is encapsulated and supported by our largest organ, our skin. Merging the two components creates a feeling of sovereignty while being connected with the world around us. As we continually remind the body that it is safe to be fully present and aware, we begin to feel more stable, whole, calm, and resourced. Our nervous system begins to relax and feel supported and safe so we may navigate everyday life with confidence and ease. Our awareness can expand and spread to the greater aspects of our lives that make us happy instead of feeling anxiety and unrest in mind and body.

To be well grounded, it is important for the mind first to set a clear intention for the body. Our physical or bodily intelligence will respond accordingly and in a powerful manner, as it will create energetic openings and pathways through the nervous system so that we may walk more solidly on this earth and be much less shaken by external challenging events we encounter.

Just as a tree takes root, it is important for us to be grounded and create stability in our lives while being fully present in each moment. When we are not rooted or grounded, we may feel that we are floating about aimlessly—and possibly get caught up in unnecessary drama and conflict. Roots make us solid. Even in the midst of external elements, just as when a tree encounters wind and rain, we can make a conscious choice to focus within ourselves and not on external influences that only have the potential to sway us. Some ways to feel grounded include being outside in nature, taking a walk, lying on the grass, swimming, or simply drinking water.

When we create the space each morning to engage ourselves in these steps, we produce profound results. We may also set the intention of having fun while creating a much stronger mind–body connection each and every day to start us on our way. It may take as little as ten minutes.

Although this book is intended primarily for children, it is equally valuable for any age group. When the initial meanings in the poems are absorbed cognitively and somatically as one, the benefit grows exponentially. I hope that children will deepen their own awareness and begin to associate feelings when seeing the illustrations, as these will become somatic bookmarks for returning them to a deeper sense of grounding.

When you lead your children through the exercises, allow them to discover the fun themselves so they will create their own personal experiences. There are no right or wrong ways to do this. Your children will find their way by the use of their bodies guiding them. Trust and allow. Amazing things will happen.

Relax your body and free all that is thought.
Let us explore grounding. First remove what was taught.

Find your special place that is quiet and free.
Perhaps it's outside and next to a tree.

Grounding is an important part of each life.
It creates the foundation to dissolve all our strife.

When we feel scattered, confused, and floating around,
Our body wants to feel safe and secure on the ground.

Allow the earth to support you in a deep, solid way.
Anchor your body as you learn how to stay.

Anchoring the body as we become more aware
Creates the stability to be free from the scare.

The mind may play tricks that are consistent with fear.
Surrender your thoughts and know you are clear.

Take a deep breath: slowly release all your worry.
Your body will relax, as there's no need to hurry.

Settled with our amazing bodies, we land.
We get to live life with all the joy in our hand.

Find a clear space with grass near a tree.
Plant your bare feet on the grass and feel solid and free.

Inside or outside won't matter so much.
Connect with the ground through sight, feeling, and touch.

Your body has always been anchored within.
The awareness of feeling is what makes you win.

Sometimes we feel scared and avoid fun things to do.
Know you are safe and grounded all the way through.

Follow the spark of excitement your body will feel.
Trust your whole body as it knows what is real.

It's not just your feet that must feel grounded and secure.
Invite your head, heart, arms, and legs to feel it much more.

All inner parts of your body, secured by your skin,
Function their best when you are grounded within.

Lead with your heart, asking your mind to relax with grace.
Feel this effortless flow and growing smile on your face.

You are solid and safe feeling fully secure.
The world is your kingdom,
playground, and more.

Inhabit your body
solidly, fluid and free.

Keep returning to feeling as you imagine your tree.

Feeling so grateful in our bodies we dwell.
We live life with much freedom when we feel all is well.

Printed in the United States
by Baker & Taylor Publisher Services